practice

John Thackway

DayOnepublications

Copyright ©Day One Publications 1996
First printed 1996

All scripture quotations are from the Authorised version.

ISBN 0902548 72 7

Published by Day One Publications
6 Sherman Road, Bromley, Kent BR1 3JH

All rights reserved

No part of this publication may be reproduced, or stored in a retrieval system, or transmitted, in any form or by any means, mechanical, electronic, photocopying, recording or otherwise, without the prior permission of **Day One Publications.**

Designed by Steve Devane. Print production by Indeprint Ltd, Bromley, Kent

Foreword

I am very pleased to be able to recommend this booklet by the Rev. John Thackway on the Lord's day. It fulfils a real need among Christians today for several reasons. Too many evangelicals have somehow picked up the false idea that God does not require us to keep any day "holy" in New Testament times. This booklet gives help on this point. Then, this booklet gives what it is hard to find almost anywhere else as far as I am aware. That is, genuine help on the practical ways in which the Lord's day is to be spent. Older books on this subject are valuable but often they assume standards in society at large which are just not found commonly in this country any more. Mr Thackway has given us all here very useful hints as to how we may make the day a delight to children even at an early age. Of course, every parent must determine before God what he and she will allow in their own home. But the suggestions here are realistic and they breathe that love of a true pastor's heart for which Mr Thackway, as a preacher and editor, is well known and loved.

MAURICE ROBERTS
Greyfriars Manse
Inverness

March 1996

How a man or woman, boy or girl uses the Lord's Day is a clear indication of where they stand regarding the day's Lord. It is their badge of either godliness or ungodliness. Sides are taken and there is no middle ground. We love God, perhaps we may say, no more than we love His day.

History informs us that the purest, brightest days of the church - especially revivals - were periods when the Lord's Day was reverenced and sanctified as part of devotion to the Lord Himself. It should be no surprise to us that *our* day of worldliness, lukewarmness and small things in the church, is also a day when godly sabbath observance is almost the exception among the Lord's people.

If we are to see a return to the great days of the past, one area that must be reformed is our use of that blessed day which comes round after every six. In this booklet are some principles to help our practice of sanctifying the Lord's day.[1] They are outlined here in order to help us welcome each seventh day and set it apart for God our Saviour.

God's day

In Scripture, repeated emphasis is placed upon the fact that this day belongs to God. For example: "...the seventh day is the sabbath of the Lord thy God" (Exodus 20:10). Expressions like this, together with others such as "my sabbaths"... "my holy day" occur around 20 times in the Old Testament. In the New Testament they are carried over in the title "the Lord's day" (Revelation 1:10). So here is a clear principle at the outset: the day we are considering is not our day, but God's. He has fenced it off from the other six days and declared it to be divine property.

We are therefore not in the realm of what we want to do on Sunday.[2] This does not come into it. Six days are generally allowed us (under God) for that. Rather, we are in the realm of what He wants us to do on Sunday. We stand on holy ground every time the day returns: the crown-rights of our God and His Christ are uppermost here. This is not to say there are no personal benefits - "the sabbath was made *for man*" (Mark 2:27) - but these come in consequence of our honouring God in a sabbath well spent for Him (Isaiah 58:13). So in considering our sabbath responsibilities, let us see ourselves as stewards entrusted with a special day. If someone lends you his property he is entitled to tell you how it is to be used, especially if it is valuable. Just so God requires in sabbath-stewards that men be found faithful (1 Corinthians 4:2).

Supposing we are permitted to live in this world for 70 years: when we stand before the Judgment Seat of Christ we shall have to give account of how we have used 3,640 Lord's days!

Nothing legalistic

There is nothing legalistic about this. If, through grace, God is our "exceeding joy" (Psalm 43:4) and we have a longing to please Him in His commandments (Psalm 119:20), then our Sunday priorities are already sorted out in our hearts. Gospel-gratitude always shows itself in willing obedience (John 14:15). The Lord's day, being a commemoration of redemption accomplished, (Deuteronomy 5:15; Mark 16:9) will draw from us a determination to give God the place such overflowing mercy deserves. Each new sabbath will find us rendering worship and loving ventures of service to Him who gave His all for us. So it is a day of unique opportunity toward our God and His dear Son. When those of us who are married were courting, and a day could be snatched to be together, we were able to fill up the day quite easily– just to have time together was enough–and the time passed all too quickly. How much more so with us and the heavenly Bridegroom of our hearts! He says to each one of us every first day of the week: "Rise up, my love, my fair one, and come away" (Song of Solomon 2:10).

Interruption

The Sabbath calls us off from the more common activities of the other six days. It is a divine and gracious interruption once in each week of life, and provides us with increased opportunities for preoccupation with godly things. Not that we should neglect these things the rest of the week. But the claims of employment and family have necessarily received the bulk of our time, attention and strength. "Sabbath" means rest, desist, cease– in order that "the one thing needful" can be attended to more largely. Sunday then, as someone has said, is "the cream of time." It is a blessed day: His kind and wise gift enabling us to indulge the desires of our renewed hearts to the full. It is only a burden and a weariness to the carnal mind for obvious reasons (see Amos 8:5; Malachi 1:13). But to the spiritually minded, God's holy day is an oasis in the desert. We are most of the way to keeping it holy if we approach it in this frame of mind. Why think in terms of what you are *not* allowed to do, when there are all the things you *are* allowed to do on Sunday? Those things we shall look at presently.

"Remember"
A good word to have before us as we consider the claims of God on His day is "Remember." It occurs right at the beginning of the fourth commandment: "Remember the sabbath day to keep it holy." It means we should bear in mind this divine ordinance, take it into account every time we make our plans, keep it in view always. We do this with our recreation and holiday arrangements. How often we have said: "Sorry, I can't make that date. We shall be away then." If such times are considered inviolable by us, how much more inviolable are God's holy-days. Therefore, what the ungodly leave until Sunday will not be left by us. For most, it is a time to do the washing, the garden, catch up with the housework, do a bit of jogging, read the newspapers, clean the car–the scrag end of the week before the start of a new week on Monday. What a manifestation of ungodliness this is! To deliberately forget the Sabbath is to rob God and raise a clenched fist in His face. Let us who profess to love and fear His name be careful in our use of His day. To avoid the encroachment of unnecessary distractions may involve a little extra thought and effort on Saturday–or earlier in the week- but where there's a will there's a way. We should keep Sunday as free as possible from mundane things that we may keep it as free as possible for God.

Lawful works
Salvation is not by works–only by virtue of our Surety's finished work (Hebrews 7:22). It is all of grace from first to last. But once saved, grace in us becomes visible in a bright array of good works (Titus 3:8; James 2:20). As someone has put it,

> *I cannot work my soul to save,*
> *For that my Lord has done;*
> *But I would work like any slave*
> *For love of God's dear Son.*

Matthew Henry said that the sabbath "is a day of holy rest that it might be a day of holy work." But what work? For ministers of the gospel and other servants of Christ the answer is clear. But what about the rest of us? We shall explore the lawful works appropriate on the sabbath day. For convenience they are broadly categorised as: Works of necessity, Works of mercy, and Works of piety.

1 Works of necessity.

Into this category come activities which are permitted because we live in this world and in human bodies. Normal life must go on and certain processes must continue, even on the Lord's day. The religion of Christ is perfectly adapted to the realities of our present situation upon earth. Beginning in the home, the preparation of food is legitimate (Matthew 12:1; Luke 14:1), although because of spiritual priorities, we will want to keep this to a minimum, having done the bulk of it some other time. On the farm or small holding, provision for livestock and pets (including veterinary work) is not prohibited on God's day (Matthew 12:11; Luke 13:15; Cf. Proverbs 12:10). And in society, because the day is a memorial of God's kindness and love, essential services such as care of the elderly, fire stations, hospital and ambulance, police, power stations and the armed forces may lawfully operate as needed. The sabbath "made for man" does not suspend the maintenance of life, health, security and comfort (John 5:9). It *does* remind us, however, that even these necessities are not what this life is all about.

2 Works of mercy.

Relieving the needy is holy work for the best day in the week. We are then imitators of the God who is rich in mercy and who delights in it (Ephesians 2:4; Micah 7:18). Our Lord healed the sick repeatedly on the Sabbath and staunchly defended His actions (e.g. Matthew 12:10-13; Luke 13:11-17; John chapters 5 and 9). What scope for serving the needs of others in His name the Sabbath affords! Visiting the sick, the lonely, the shut-ins (James 1:27). Opening our home and table to other believers (1 Peter 4:9); remembering to avoid the Martha-syndrome, which can be counter-productive (Luke 10:40-42). And, of course, the spreading of God's saving Word–the highest work of mercy we can possibly do. Sunday School teaching, tract distribution, prison visiting, open-air preaching and the like. All this is work to make angels envious.

3 Works of piety.

Attending the house of God (which will be considered below) is chief among the works of piety. Also the more private duties of reading, prayer and spiritual conversation. The training of our children at home to love the Lord's day, and their training in church, is also included and will be discussed later.

With all this to fill up each sabbath, it is surprising that Christians should find any problem with what to do on this day. If our aim is to please the God we love, and if we have before us the principles and priorities outlined above, where would be the time (let alone the divine permission) for television, radio, the beach, shops, restaurants, newspapers, chores, hobbies, excursions and sport?

Divine worship
If the "daily round" of each sabbath is likened to a circular crown, and the various spiritual privileges to so many jewels, then divine worship is the choice diamond, the Koh-i-noor. Assembled with Christ's church, we reach the pinnacle of all Lord's day sanctification. Nothing else we do is better than this. The sung praises of God, prayer, the reading and preaching of God's Word, the communion of saints–to spend time devoted to these things is sabbath-keeping par excellence! No wonder David could cry, "For a day in thy courts is better than a thousand," and the writer to the Hebrews warned, "Not forsaking the assembling of ourselves together, as the manner of some is" (Psalm 84:10; Hebrews 10:25). It is noteworthy in the annals of church history that whenever God visited His people in revival, meetings and services multiplied and lengthened: Christians could not spend enough time together with God. This was conspicuously true on the Lord's day, when morning, afternoon and evening services reflected the belief that this was the finest way to keep the day set apart for God. Alas, what is to be said for the multitude of modern "oncers," who consider a single service on the Lord's day enough? Apart from weakening the numerical strength of the service and discouraging the pastor, such people betray a deplorably low view of God, His Word, His people and His day. The question such absentees need to be asked is: "How *do* you spend the time on the Lord's day that is not spent in the house of God?"

Examples
There are many scriptural examples of those who "called the sabbath a delight" by diligent attendance at public worship. Our Lord Himself "as his custom was, went into the synagogue on the sabbath day" (Luke 4:16). If any Christian baulks at the *habit* of weekly church attendance, let him note the ultimate Example: "as his custom was." When our Lord intimated the change of day from the seventh to the first day of the week, He did it by visiting the little assemblies of His disciples the same evening (John 20:19-29). Although not strictly meetings for worship,

they quickly became so by the presence and revelation of the living Lord in their midst. How often in our experience the same thing in principle has been granted us, and we would not have missed those times for anything (Matthew 18:20).

The book of Acts gives us glimpses of meetings convened on the Lord's Day. For example: "And upon the first day of the week, when the disciples came together to break bread, Paul preached unto them" (Acts 20:7). When writing to the church at Corinth, Paul gives directions about the collection for the saints at Jerusalem. He envisages them meeting on the first day of the week and urges them to lay aside their contributions then (1 Corinthians 16:1,2). And, of course, it was on that unforgettable Lord's day that the apostle was "in the Spirit" and received such glorious manifestations of the exalted Christ (Revelation 1:10-20).

Later church history affords similar glimpses. Origen, the learned Alexandria Scholar, who lived 185-254 AD, wrote:

"Therefore relinquishing Judaical observances of the Sabbath, let us see of what sort the observance ought to be to the Christian. On the day of the Sabbath it behoves us that nothing of all worldly works should be done. If, therefore, you cease from all secular employment, and carry on nothing worldly, and are at leisure for spiritual occupation, and go to church, giving ear to the reading and treating of the divine Word, and think of heavenly things, and are solicitous about the future hope, and have before your eyes the coming judgment, and have not respect for present and visible things, but to the unseen and future–this is the observance of the Christian Sabbath."

Matthew Henry was distinguished for his love of the Lord's day. He once remarked that "God is jealous concerning His Sabbaths; and that to sanctify them is a part of the character of a good Christian." When recovering from an illness, he said: "It is comfortable to reflect upon an affliction borne patiently; an enemy forgiven heartily; and a sabbath sanctified uprightly." Such a man, we might expect, would have something helpful to say about public worship on the Sabbath day:

"Keep close to the God of grace. Ordinances (worship, the preached Word etc.–J.P. Thackway.) are the golden pipes by which the oil of grace is conveyed. That holy oil keeps the lamp of hope burning; therefore

*David desires to **dwell** in the house of the Lord all the days of his life. Let sanctuary privileges make you long to be within the veil."*

Friendly directions

However, not every kind of attendance at Lord's day worship glorifies God and does us good. Our mere presence at the means of grace does not necessarily mean that grace will come to us. There are some conditions to meet if God is to meet with us. Here are some "Friendly directions" adapted from a piece written in the last century by a godly clergyman, Ashton Oxenden:-

1. Always go to God's house *expecting a blessing*. Look out for it, and especially ask for it. Go in a devout spirit. Before you leave your home, pause for a moment or two, and beg of the Lord to prepare your heart by His Holy Spirit, and enable you to worship Him as you ought.

2. When there, *enter with all your heart into the service*. In prayer, let your heart join with your fellow-worshippers as well as your minister. It is not enough to sit quietly while your minister sends up his petitions to heaven; but *pray the prayers yourself*. Yes, pray them with all your heart.

3. When God's Word is read, *listen with your whole attention*. It may be you have often heard those chapters before, or read them yourself; but they contain precious truths, which are always new to the hearing ear and the understanding heart.

4. During the sermon, *be a humble listener*. You should be as a little child, feeling that your knowledge is but small, and that you have much to learn. You should be like a hungry man who comes to be fed, seeking to get your soul nourished by the bread of life. You should be like the thirsty soil, which waits to drink in the falling shower. If we all heard in this way, who can tell what blessings would flow from every service, and how many would come away from this ordinance of God filled and refreshed? Perhaps you are growing deaf, and can only pick up a part of what is said by the preacher. Perhaps too, your memory fails you, when you gather up what you have heard. Still, you can carry away something; and you will be thankful for that something, if you feel that it is a part of God's own message.

5. Another direction I will give you. *When you come home from the house of God,* do not forget the service in which you have been engaging. Converse about it, if you have an opportunity. Get out your Bible and find the text; and then talk over any part of the sermon which you can remember. This is the way to refresh your memory, and to lay up a store of spiritual knowledge.

Absence
Mention must now be made of absenting ourselves from God's house on His day. So far we have seen that two constraints ensure we are in our place there: spiritual desire and scriptural duty. When we are missing, one (or both) of these is involved: desire is weak or duty is neglected. If we find ourselves away from divine worship *for no valid reason,*[3] then our absence says something about the state of our soul. Whatever excuses we may satisfy our conscience with, before the Lord we have none. He sees affections that are not toward Him as before; He sees a disregard of His revealed will. Forsaking the assemblies of saints on the Lord's day is not so much a condition as a symptom of something else. There is an underlying condition which is manifesting itself. We should examine ourselves to see what is wrong with us. Those who love the Lord become backsliders in heart first (Proverbs 14:14), before openly straying from the paths of godliness. Each of us needs this self-admonition: "Keep thy heart with all diligence; for out of it are the issues of life" (Proverbs 4:23).

Common problem
A common problem for many Christians today is when ungodly friends or relatives visit them on Sunday. What happens to church then? A dilemma is created: do I still go to church and risk offending my visitors– or do I miss church (just for once) and entertain the guests who have paid me the compliment of visiting my home? This is not necessarily a straightforward question to answer. If, for instance, the wife is a Christian and the husband is not, she does not have full control of the situation. Neither have sons or daughters whose parents are not the Lord's. There are complications, too, when we are visited by married children who have not come to faith in Christ.

These, and others, are special cases needing special wisdom, and the Lord promises to guide his perplexed children (Psalm 25:9; James 1:5). In some cases it may be prudent to remain at home with these guests– in others, a stand may have to be made. Each case is unique and it is for the Lord to direct every time.

But if we are favoured with a Christian home, what then? Here are some pointers toward an answer. **First,** we should avoid the situation ever arising. Earlier we mentioned the need to "remember" the Sabbath: to keep it in mind when making our arrangements etc. If we convey to would-be visitors that we always go to church on Sundays, then we have made our position clear beforehand and they will know the score. **Secondly,** we must realise that the claims of God on His day are more important than the claims of ungodly visitors. This is the principle embedded in the fourth commandment. Why feel guilty about politely saying to them that you must be leaving now for church? The world does not abandon its leisure plans when they have unexpected visitors. Can you imagine a football fan deciding not to go and support his team just because a friend has called who is not interested in the game? I imagine it would be a case of: "Either come with me to the match or I'll see you another time"! **Thirdly,** if we show ourselves willing to forsake our sacred appointments with God we are a poor witness. We are saying that He is dispensable in our lives when something (apparently) more important turns up on a Sunday. This will not impress our friends and relatives with the vital necessity of seeking God in Christ for themselves. Let us tactfully and graciously honour God on His day. He will honour our right priorities and take care of all the consequences.

The measure in which Scriptural sanctification of the Lord's day is revived will be the measure in which our churches are strengthened, personal godliness increased and the world not allowed to overlook how glorious it is to be a Christian.

> *Take my life, and let it be*
> *Consecrated, Lord, to Thee;*
> *Take my moments and my days,*
> *Let them flow in ceaseless praise.*

Children, Church and the Lord's Day
The question of what to do with children on the Lord's day is of special concern to Christian parents. Our bringing them up "in the nurture and admonition of the Lord" (Ephesians 6:4) must include training them to sanctify this day along with us. "Thou...thy son...thy daughter" is included in the 4th Commandment (Exodus 20:10). But how can we achieve this? And what practical steps can we take toward helping our children love the Lord's day?

Let us be careful to avoid wrong thinking here. Because our children will be unregenerate in their early years we may be tempted to feel that we cannot expect them to treat Sunday as we do. That would be "imposing our standards upon them." But such fears run counter to the Ten Commandments themselves, which are for the unregenerate also, and are a stepping-stone to the gospel (Galatians 3:24). Moreover, as Christian parents, we are to *"command* our children to keep the way of the Lord" (Genesis 18:19), therefore we do not impose *our* standards upon them but *God's*. So we have divine warrant for setting this standard in the home, and happy the children who are brought up in the physical, mental and spiritual privileges of the Lord's day there.

Example
What, then, should we do with our youngsters on Sabbath days? It cannot be stressed too much the place our example has in this. Children learn by imitation long before they listen to our teaching. If we obviously love God's holy day in the weekly rhythm of home-life, the foundation is being laid for our children to follow us in this habit of godliness.

Parents have two kinds of authority: their lips which command, and their example which commends.

General points
Before coming to more practical matters, a few general points should be made. **First,** small children are not adults. They are little people whose God-given instincts are all in the direction of play and physical expression. This is taken very seriously by them. Through these things much of their early learning comes. This obviously has to be borne in mind when ordering the Sabbath observance of the home. To cut right across these natural and innocent traits in our expectations may be putting a yoke upon them which the Lord will not own. I am not advocating the free use of toys and games, but I am cautioning against an unimaginative and stultifying approach which forgets the age and capacities of our little ones.

Second, children differ from each other quite markedly. There are many variables: age, temperament, intelligence, physical energy and so on. Therefore, what may be helpful for one child may not be for another. God lays it upon the head of the household to administer the Sabbath realistically and wisely. We need to plead with God for the guidance He has promised (Psalm 32:8; James 1:5).

Third, Children do need to be provided for on the Lord's day. When at home it can be sheer laziness and abdication of responsibility to just "give them something to do" to keep them quiet. This will probably neither satisfy them nor teach them the positive blessings of this day. Paradoxically, occupying children and training them to use the day aright can be hard work! But it is a spiritual investment which will bring an eternal reward.

Fourth, we must make it clear that "neutral" activities are not good enough on God's day. The perversity of little minds will often try to skirt round the obligation by saying, "But Daddy, playing such and such is not exactly unholy." To which the reply must be, "No, son, but it is not exactly holy either." In other words, it is not *the absence of the ungodly element* that makes a Sabbath activity legitimate, *it is the presence of the godly element*. This must be always our aim on the Sabbath of the Lord "in all our dwellings" (Leviticus 23:3).

Family Worship
Family worship will set the tone of the Lord's day for parents and children. Breakfast devotions, with the extra time available, can be hallowed and directed toward the rest of the day. In many ways, the battle to succeed with our children on the Sabbath will be won or lost here. Parents who get up too late for this are setting a bad example and will inflict spiritual loss upon the household (see Proverbs 20:13). If children are used to family worship at home–especially Sunday morning–they will readily take to the discipline of sitting quietly in church and worshipping there. Our childrens' behaviour in church will reflect their experience of the equivalent at home. These days we are seeing increasingly the spectacle of children disrupting divine worship by their noisiness and inability to sit still, and the worse spectacle of parents helplessly trying to contain the situation. Perhaps worst of all is that so many of God's people seem to regard this as normal. This certainly would not have been the case a few generations ago. It has more to do with the neglect of parents concerning family worship and the discipline of children than with normality (see Proverbs 13:24; 19:18; 22:15; 23:13,14; 29:15,17).

Children in church
Let us examine what the Bible has to say about the place of children in the public worship of God. Much modern thinking would tell us that we cannot expect younger ones to sit through our "adult" services. Various

devices are therefore employed to make it more bearable for them. Short, entertaining "childrens' talks" are the most common. These generally take the form of entertaining anecdotes with little biblical content, and sometimes all they do is make the children (and adults) laugh and thus lower the tone of the whole service. In some churches a creche system operates for children up to secondary school age; in others the Sunday School runs at the same time as the morning service, thus removing the children altogether. Even in churches where these practices are not found, some parents allow their children to play with toys during the sermon or read books.

All these concessions betray an unbiblical view of the public worship of God. They are out of accord with what the Lord requires of parents and children in the solemn assemblies. When Israel were gathered before Moses to hear God's Word, we read: "Ye stand this day all of you before the LORD your God...*your little ones*, your wives" (Deuteronomy 29:10,11; see also Joshua 8:35; 2 Chronicles 20:13). There is no hint anywhere in the Old Testament that children were removed from such gatherings–or that alternative provision was made for them.[4] God expected complete families to be in His presence on such occasions.

In the Gospels it is clear that children were among the multitudes who followed our Lord around and listened to His teaching. One lad among His hearers provided a meal that was miraculously multiplied to feed 5,000 (John 6:9). Jesus suddenly drew a child from the people to give His disciples an object-lesson in humility (Matthew 18:2). At another time mothers brought their children to Him for His blessing–children who had immediately before been His hearers (Mark 10:1,13-16). And children were quite clearly among His audience when He cleansed the temple (Matthew 21:12-16).

The Epistles, too, are illuminating on this point. Paul writing to the Ephesians and Colossians specifically addresses children (Ephesians 6:1; Colossians 3:20). These letters would be read to the assembled church in someone's house by the elders. In the Ephesian letter he has a word for "wives" (5:22), "husbands" (5:25), and then he says: "Children, obey your parents in the Lord..." (6:1). And similarly in Colossians. Paul expected children to be present for the "sermon" and to hear his words to *them*. Here is apostolic proof that the congregation must not be fragmented, but that whole families should worship the Lord and hear His Word together.

Creche, of course, is a help for babies and toddlers–not to say parents! But by school age, and really even before then, children should have been lovingly but firmly trained in the discipline of being present throughout divine worship. Our expectations of children in this matter tend to be far too low. They are more capable than we realise of being still and being quiet, of understanding some of what they hear, and of receiving spiritual grace. Did not God speak to Samuel? God will honour parental faithfulness in this area more than we are prepared to believe.

Hospitality
Having arrived home from church and the children boisterous, what can we do to occupy them, satisfying their needs and the requirements of the Lord's day? The ministry of hospitality (Romans 12:13; 1 Peter 4:9) is a great help here. The presence of godly friends gives youngsters others to talk with who will augment our example and influence. Let this be a reminder to those privileged to share the homes of Christian families: what the children see in us, and hear from us, is so important. May we be guests who underline not undermine, what parents are seeking to inculcate. Many testimonies contain reference to the good effect godly visitors had upon younger members of the family. One father told me recently that he attributed, under God, the conversion of all his children to the regular practice of having the Lord's people for meals and in his home.

Spiritual talk
Mealtimes are a good opportunity to encourage conversation along spiritual lines. If it was morning Sunday School, questions can be asked about the lesson. Children can also be gently coaxed to see what they can remember of the sermon. Such natural reference to the things of God sanctifies meals and enhances the effect of having been under the Word (see Deuteronomy 6:7). The meal over, and while still around the table, what a good opportunity to sing a psalm or hymn, and for father to lead in prayer, giving thanks for another meal enjoyed, for the blessings of the Lord's day, and a request that the family might always remember to keep it holy. Questions often come from little ones at such times (Deuteronomy 6:20) and answering them is all part of the privilege of "not speaking thine own words" when "calling the Sabbath a delight" (Isaiah 58:13).

Practical suggestions
The afternoon of the Lord's day is probably the time when most work needs to be done in the family. If there is afternoon Sunday School this helps greatly. But let us suppose there is not and a longish stretch of the day lies before us until tea time. How to fill this up profitably is not easy. Here are some specific suggestions:-

1 For most children, simply to have their parents' attention will be their greatest pleasure. For Mum and Dad to sit down with them and talk about their concerns–guiding them to think in a biblical way–can be so fruitful. The trouble with many parents (including Christian ones) is that they scarcely know how to spend *any* day or time with their children. What a golden opportunity the gift of the Lord's day provides!

2 Reading younger children "Sunday books" is another helpful occupation. In the English-speaking world we are favoured with a wide range of them, although not all are suitable. We should go for those based upon the biblical text and which illuminate doctrine. *The Child's Story Bible, Leading Little Ones to God* (Banner of Truth), and the Christian Focus range *Miracles and Parables of Jesus* (Gospel Standard Publications) are excellent examples.

3 Bible colouring books can be a useful variation. The *Trinitarian Bible Society* produce very fine outline texts for colouring and learning. The *Lord's Day Observance Society* also publish similar materials. Those who have done the best coloured-in ones can have them displayed in the room and our children will feel they have made us attractive motto text cards.

4 Taking children through a catechism is another excellent occupation for a while on the Lord's day. There are some good ones available for use with children. I have found the *Catechism for Young People*[5] very suitable. This consists of 140 questions and answers. This is a time-honoured way to impart doctrinal instruction to young minds.

5 *Pilgrim's Progress* has stood families in good stead for centuries. After the Bible, this, together with *Foxe's Book of Martyrs,* used to be staple reading for children on Sunday afternoons. It would be good to have today's rising generation acquainted with these spiritual classics once more. There are several childrens' editions of *Pilgrim's Progress* available, but like the story Bible, choose one that adheres closely to the original text so that youngsters can graduate to the full version later. Bunyan's allegory is full of characters that readily appeal to children and is an excellent and even entertaining book to read to or with them.

6 If any of the family can play a suitable instrument, accompanied hymn singing can lift the spirit and sanctify some of the Lord's day afternoon. This traditional custom has so much to commend it, but care must be taken that it rises above the level of a "sing-song." Whenever we employ the voice in hymns and psalms we ascribe praise to the infinite and exalted God–even in a more informal situation. We must guard against irreverence in our own house, just as much as in God's house (1 Timothy 3:15).

7 Going out for a short walk is felt by some families a fine way of meeting the physical and spiritual needs of children on Sunday. Admiring the beauties of creation and sharing the intimacies of family conversation can be a hallowed occupation. Isaac went out into the field to prayerfully meditate (Genesis 24:63). And on the Sabbath our Lord and His disciples walked and talked together (Matthew 12:1). If this is kept from degenerating into just a Sunday afternoon stroll, "a walk thus improved may be a walk to heaven, and is very consistent with walking with God" (John Willison).

Ministers of the gospel

Let us particularly pray for Ministers who are family men in all of this. Having the same responsibility toward their children, they do not have the same Sabbath rest as others. After the nervous energy expended in the pulpit, sometimes the last thing they feel like is reading to lively youngsters. Still feeling wound up, or cast down–and anticipating the evening service–what grace they need!

Let us also pray for the Pastor's wife. Sometimes her husband has to finish sermon preparation on Sunday afternoon, or is even out preaching at that time. This means the children are solely her responsibility, which can be extremely wearing. She, who has borne the brunt of the childrens' needs during the week, sometimes gets scant relief on the Lord's day–the day when she cannot just send them out to play with the neighbour's children. And if she has the added work of hospitality, the pressures can be great indeed. Lord's days in the manse involve a unique sacrifice–may our readers often remember the occupants before the throne of heavenly grace (Hebrews 4:15,16).

Conclusion

As I close, no one can write on a subject like this without reflecting upon his own performance over the years. How many shortcomings and failures I feel I have to confess! As a family, we have not always succeeded in consistently implementing the principles and practices of this booklet. But I can also say that, as grace has been given, we anticipate the Lord's Day with pleasure. And I believe our spending those days together as we do enriches our family life immeasurably, and contributes to the measure of spiritual blessing each of us knows. May we all seek to recover family religion in these degenerate times, and loudly proclaim with God's servant of old, "as for me and my house, we will serve the LORD" (Joshua 24:15).

Notes

1 For a study on the relationship between the Old Testament sabbath and the New Testament Lord's day, see my booklet *The Lord's Day–Special or Sabbath?* Lord's Day Observance Society, 1988. It is available from LDOS headquarters, 6 Sherman Road, Bromley, Kent BR1 3JH for 45p.

2 I use the word "Sunday" purely for convenience. It has no foundation in Scripture as a name for God's day. The origin of the word is in the Dies solis "day of the sun" of the Roman calendar, which was the first day of the week and dedicated to the sun. It is easy to see how some early Christians re-interpreted this in terms of the rising of "the Sun of righteousness" (Malachi 4:2). Its official connection with the Lord's day seems to stem from the edict of the roman emperor Constantine in 321 AD, which required "rest on the venerable day of the sun." From this pagan, Christianised sun-day has come the term we now know as Sunday.

3 In saying this, exception must be made of those who genuinely cannot be present at Lord's day assemblies for worship. Ill health, providential circumstances beyond our control, etc. are reasons which can be offered to God. Included in the latter are, sadly, the growing number of believers who love the public means of grace but who no longer find themselves within reach of a spiritually-sound local church. Such is the departure from "the old paths" these days that once-faithful churches can change quickly, and in so doing exclude some of their best people. Our hearts go out to the numbers of believers isolated in this way. We feel for those who long to be present in a church where reverence, submission to Scripture, love of the brethren and spiritual worship characterise the gatherings. May the Lord somehow give them the desire of their hearts!

4 If Nehemiah 8:2 is cited ("men and women, and all that could hear with understanding"), it must be remembered that here was an exceptional and historic occasion.

The Jews had been restored from Captivity and they had gathered to hear the law of God read and expounded to them once again. This was not part of the regular assemblies of God's people, where all were normally present. In understanding the Scriptures, we do not make a rule out of an exception.

5 Available from: Hayes Town Chapel Evangelical Church, St. Marys Road, Hayes, Middlesex.